Fani Papageorgiou

Fani Papageorgiou

When You Said No,
Did You Mean
Never?

Shearsman Books

First published in the United Kingdom in 2013 by
Shearsman Books
50 Westons Hill Drive
Emersons Green
BRISTOL
BS16 7DF

Shearsman Books Ltd Registered Office
30–31 St. James Place, Mangotsfield, Bristol BS16 9JB
(this address not for correspondence)

www.shearsman.com

ISBN 978-1-84861-265-5

Contents

When You Said No,
Did You Mean Never?

The Riddle

Around the 1840s, a Danish traveller to Hamburg, Count Schimmelmann, happened to come upon a small itinerant Menagerie, and to take a fancy to it. One day Count Schimmelmann was sunk in contemplation of the Hyena, when the proprietor of the Menagerie came and addressed him.

'Your Excellency does well to look at the Hyena,' said he. 'It is a great thing to have got a Hyena to Hamburg, where there has never been one till now. All Hyenas, you will know, are hermaphrodites, and in Africa, where they come from, on a full-moon night they will meet and join in a ring of copulation wherein each individual takes the double part of male and female. Did you know that?'

'No,' said Count Schimmelmann with a slight movement of disgust.

'Do you consider now, your Excellency,' said the showman, 'that it should be, on account of this fact, harder for a Hyena than for other animals to be shut up by itself in a cage? Would he feel a double want, or is he, because he unites in himself the complementary qualities of creation, satisfied in himself, and in harmony?

In other words, since we are all prisoners in life, are we happier, or more miserable, the more talents we possess?'

Dark Matter

In physics we call it dark
because it doesn't radiate.

In Greece it can be stork nests in the bell tower,
moss on the flagstones,
a dull pain in the sky.

Ovid

There is a story
that friends visited him one day
and begged him to remove
three disastrous lines from his vast *oeuvre*.

'Certainly,' he replied
'but there are three lines
that I will not remove'
and the selections
were of course identical.

Do not ask how many miles you have gone.
No, ask how many remain.

Bleach

All you need is egg whites, vinegar and soap flakes
We're obsessed with getting it right.
All pure honey will granulate
and you can make anything you want.

During the First World War, pits from olives,
peaches, prunes, cherries, dates and plums
became carbon for gas masks.

Longing

She calls it something blue.
I call it Andrew Carnegie
controlling the price of steel.
Walking down the street
knowing there is one person
you have to live without.

Life is tenuous
and there will be glassware in her chest.
Write down what you love.

Hapax Legomenon

A word that occurs only once
in a language's recorded texts
or in an author's body of work.

I'm waiting for something to happen,
thought Cordelia,
and then it did.
Lear speaks of shadowy forests and plenteous rivers
but never discloses where his palace lies.
We imagine the logs freshly hewn,
the china blue sky.

Someone always wants you to give up,
thought Cordelia,
and she just couldn't stop walking.

You heavens, give me that patience,
patience I need, says Lear,
every inch a king.
Come on, let's ruin each other's lives,
says Cordelia.

Legend

Constantine Paleologus, the last Byzantine Emperor was not killed when Constantinople fell to the Turks in 1453 but disappeared into a wall and will return when the time is right to retake Constantinople.

Karen learns about it in primary school.
This is when she starts to notice
empty space is affected by gravity
when she can only go ahead
by avoiding cracks on the pavement
her feet close enough to the cleft
for the racket in her head to go away
and for the first time she hears silence
as if the streets were laid with straw
the way the palace guards had muted the sound
at Queen Victoria's funeral.

Stating the Obvious

The sky appears blue during the day because of a process known as Rayleigh scattering. More of the blue light reaches us than other colours in the spectrum.

People see what they feel on everything around them—on the houses and trees and poles and power lines and mostly in the sky.

Almost everything happens in language.

The Mood

Isn't the genetic language of all life the same?
The sea that laps the town
the man who casts everyone aside
the girl waiting on a bench with empty hands
the water in the ocean—choppy and full of shadows
the dreams where kestrels are eating up the sun
any single life which reaches the middle so quickly—

what diminishes constraint diminishes strength.

Tea Stains on Cups

A cloth sprinkled with salt,
that's all you need,
her grandmother said.
One day you have to learn to keep house.

Don't leave smears on objects.
Remember Virgil, her mother said,
there are tears in things.

We Know Now America and India Are Different Places

Ask me anything you want.
There is no blood in a stone.
A camel can walk fifty kilometres without water.
A man's life lasts less than thirty thousand days.

It is our solemn privilege
to decide never to heal.

Talk to me a thousand times.

Begin at the Beginning Then

It resembles the Mariana Trench in the Pacific,
the deepest place in any ocean.
If you dropped a one-kilo rock in the water there,
it would take an hour to reach the seabed.

The bottoms of deep trenches
are completely dark.

Verbal Reasoning

What goes uphill and downhill
but never moves?
Come on, stay with problems longer.
A road.

Bridges get slightly longer
as they heat up in the sun.
Heat can make a person crazy.
People with brown eyes
can have blue-eyed children.

This is the hurt which drives everyone mad.
A life is a life is a life.

Sex

A monsoon is a wind
that blows one way all summer
and the other way all winter.

She closes every door gently
pulling with one hand, pushing with the other
her eyes wide and clear.

Gibbon kept the sexual escapades of the looser Romans
in the original Latin
like quicksilver in loaves of bread.

An Interjection

It is not grammatically related
to any other part of the sentence.
It is added to convey emotion.
Hey, I can't do this anymore.

We wear out our lungs with talking.
This is the place where she loses her voice.

She drowns in the life she lives in her mind,
while cliffs are worn back,
roads and towns are falling into the sea.

Marasmus

In Greek it is the depletion
of physical and emotional strength

due to prolonged illness or unhappiness,
despondency or simply a heavy heart.

In medicine it signifies
a condition of progressive wasting away.

The wine is someone else's
but the glass is ours,

a Greek proverb goes.

Reduction

In chemistry it is
when a substance loses oxygen.
In all other circumstances,
it is when a thing is made smaller
or less in amount.

With love it's both.

The Gesture

His house was opposite hers.
He spent all his time pacing the balcony.
How are you, he yelled at her
the minute she turned the corner
walking home from school every afternoon.
He adjusted his thick glasses and waved his hand
as if she were already in a boat.
My best regards to your parents and your brother, he said.
Why doesn't he go to school, she screamed at home,
why does he talk like that, why does he never put a shirt on—
but no one gave her any answers.

Hey, she yelled as she was opening the garden gate,
how's it going?
With nothing decided yet
With the love that she still has in her
The burden of many waters
Karen smiles and waves back with all her strength
as if he, too, is in a boat
and just before pushing the key into the main door,
tiny wings flapping against her blood,
she glances up where he is pacing up and down
and looks at his vest and bony shoulders
and knows she'll never forget him.

The Language

Goodbye my love,
someone will write on her chemistry book
and she will read it before she goes to bed
and it will go straight on her solar plexus and stay there
Click... click

You give away your power too easily,
someone will say under a corrugated pink sky,
on a tiny island off the west coast of Scotland
and she will have nowhere to go
Click... click

I must not see you again under the circumstances,
someone will say looking at the carpet
and she will start bleeding into her own brain
Click... click

Come here, you
someone will say at a party
You and I robbed a bank together in another life
and like the growth rings on a tree,
her adult life will begin without her knowing it
and it will proceed in circles, from within outwards.
But first she will have to find a voice.

Absolute Zero

In 1848 Lord Kelvin developed a temperature scale with zero set at the limit of molecular motion.

By the time they read about him at school
Karen is navigating streets choked with fallen trees.

The Glasgow Coma Scale

I've wasted my life,
her grandfather said,
don't waste yours.

It is a common saying
that a man needs only six feet of earth
that hens do not sleep at night
that a hero cannot recover his lost beloved
until he wears out a pair of iron shoes.

Life is accident and organic matter
her grandfather said.
An ache under her breastbone
as if something were ending right that minute.

The Involvement

Gone is the study of birds' entrails,
Exit the tapestry weavers of Antwerp,
the pound with the dogs,
long hotel afternoons,
the edge of a camphor forest.

Don't fuss, dear heart,
her mother used to say
There are vitamins in the sun.

The Knowledge

*In Modern Greek words end mostly in vowels; when they do end in
consonants, it can be either "n" or "s" and nothing else.*

She has been standing in the middle of this for so long now
Like lying at the bottom of a crevasse
with both legs broken.

I will tell you everything,
a Greek expression goes,
including the "n" and the "s"
You... she whispers
as she swims in the ocean.

It takes eighty-eight laps
to make a mile.

Letters

Her life consists of red and blue edges of air-mail envelopes
Now, do without me
He had written.

For less than half a second
she's going to drop everything and run.
Make it fast, Karen.

A Light at the End of Your Dock

Gatsby had bought that house
so Daisy would be just across the bay.
Karen wonders if people measure distance
in miles or minutes.

She knows that her hands
will not only crack books
and open jars
but also throw endless small stones
towards the reeds
at the edges of rivers.

Mark a place inside you
and name it the dock,
she says every night.
She enters the dark kitchen
smelling of tea and lemons.

With shadows under her eyes
and much diminished
she stays in bed all day.

Nothing is holding together.
The tilt of the world is humming in her blood.

The Method of Trial and Error

Why do you keep slamming doors on my fingers—
Really, why do you?

Yes, life is like that.
You're warm with sex still in your eyes
And you speed up my heart.

Due to Lack of Interest
Tomorrow Has Been Cancelled

What's the hardest thing for you—
To want the wrong thing or wondering where to go?
Is grief simply maddening
or just lakeshore lost to erosion?

We begin to store happiness.
What we don't eat in season
We're canning for the winter.

We could collapse a mine together
or hold back the sea.
So which one is love?

Paper, Scissors, Stone

Paper beats stone (as it can wrap it up)
Children who ring the doorbell and then run away

Stone beats scissors (as it can blunt them)
Clerks writing in ledgers in a meticulous slow hand

Scissors beat paper (as they can cut it)
Assyrian emperors sending parcels of human ears.

Oubliette

A secret dungeon
with access only through a ceiling trapdoor.
Those with a full night's sleep behind them
whose chests are never punched black and blue
rarely go there.

Time was the only thing Gatsby could not fix.
Do you always watch for the longest day of the year
and then miss it? Daisy asks.
Knock once for yes, twice for no.

Monopoly

Don't sell your railroads,
her grandfather warned her.
He was the race car,
her brother was the shoe
and she was the thimble.

The smell of oatmeal and antiseptic from the kitchen.
You wonder how many things in the world
deserve your loyalty, Karen.
Well can't you see I have cake in my mouth?

I'll tell you something
if you promise not to get mad—
All you need is a strong sense of what is fitting.
Facts are shadows of rabbits made by hands on the wall.
They smell like burnt mineral.
They are only as strong as China tea but
they'll fill your shoes with silver and gold.

Walking

Your feet should always face *en dehors*,
her mother said.
It requires energy and resolve
to tread from point A to point B.
The world is resilient.

Everything she knows about life
and about people who go straight to bed after supper
is that they wear down
until they can't wear down anymore.
She has tried to create a lake out of nothing.

So where is it?
Yugoslavia isn't really a place any more.
The Bible should be read for its poetry
not its dogma.
A quart is a unit of liquid capacity.
You can break everyone's heart
but you can't break the furniture.
Look again Karen.
Let the iron in your blood be the dowser's twitch—
the treasure is not on the table.

Keep walking in your bad shoes
crowding your feet with their ingots of silver and gold.
Darling, little fish-bone, where have you been?

Haunted House

Dogs biting her
being thirsty but finding no water
and being in one room
and then another and another
always full of people and never alone.
Yearning is an airshaft coated in wet sand.
Cleaning the eavestrough never helps.

Her grandmother dreams of the knife grinder
pushing his cart round the streets
as he did when she was growing up on a small Greek island.
At his cry, housewives brought down their knives
to be ground on his wheel.

Grammatical Moods

They describe a verb's relationship to reality and intent.
We had a life together, then all hell broke loose.

She has a feeling in her bones
that nothing is ever said once,
that she will have this conversation so many times.

That one day
she will let all the houseplants die
and jump in the water
to try and find a crack in the seabed
beneath the Atlantic
and she will still have her coat on,
forgetting altogether
how heavy winter clothes can be.

And she will find that the people who interest her
are the ones who are not clear despite themselves
and she will spend time with them
just wandering on the water's edge
and she will have crackers in her pockets
and leave her light on at night.

How to Iron a Shirt

Collar, yoke, cuffs, sleeves, back, front.
When will you learn to be a wife, they asked.

We have an extra kidney,
an extra lung,
extra teeth
but only one
disposition.

The Basilisk

The ice on the pavement has its grain
fog is cloud very near the ground.
Things are less easy to love.

The way water spots form on the ceiling
no two people wear down in the same places.

The world is cold water pipes
and animals in pastures
and we stand warned.
The world is an ancient catacomb
containing bones and skulls
and migration is only
a way of coping with the tilt.

What is holding us back
has the deepest roots
and according to Pliny
she is a monster
a tiny darkness
causing death by a single glance.

Modal Verbs

I may
I must
I can
They express
how likely or possible
an event is.
They pare things down.

Hey Karen
you have the legacy of waste in your bones
but we all inherit everything.
The light in the shipyards
the lindens that start to end
evening on the surface of the lake.
There is a piece of whalebone
stuck in the depths of your eye sockets
but it is we who choose what to cherish
and what to disavow.

Then get what you want
and you're ruined.

Why. Won't. You. Talk to Me.

The world becomes a different place
when people start washing their hands.
People who keep gas bills from years and years ago.
The rain worries them.
They look at the ceiling, they look at the floor.
They take down the curtains, wash, bleach and iron them.
They nest all the spoons and forks in the silverware tray.
They lie in bed all night listening to the express trains go by.
The world doesn't know what's best for them—
there is nothing to love.

She is part of the heavy waters that pound the coast all winter.
She congregates with shadows in whatever part is darkest.
She calls and whispers, pick up, pick up, talk to me.
She gets no answer and no answer.
She dilutes nothing.

There are people with baseball on the brain.
Purpose lining the four chambers of their hearts
birds nesting in their hair
but nonetheless, they pick up an instrument.

It's Better with the Cracks

Influenza viruses come from birds not humans;
even cold lakes get sick because of them.

The man who stepped out for a paper
and never came back
lives inside us all.

Opening a Jar

Insert a small spoon
between the lid and the jar
to break the vacuum.
No wonder people do this.

There would be no back-and-forth in her life
no aimless lingering
no two shoes that were not fellows.

Mr. Crusoe Senior told his son
to preserve his watchword;
a place for everything
and everything in its place.

Most young people look as if
they are going to do something
by the time they are thirty.
Without bones, she could slide under the door.

Dead Man's Fingers

Any scientist will tell you that there is gold in the water
but it costs too much to collect it.
Still, there is gold in the water
and while she saved her money in canning jars
she began to look for smooth stones in the sea
and definitions in language—
Swiss cheese is an American cheese with holes in it;
A *water clock* uses the flow of water to measure time;
Dead-man's-fingers is a soft coral with spongy lobes
stiffened by calcareous spines;
and she knew then that when found
washed up on the beach
it would resemble the fingers of a corpse
and that she could wait
but she couldn't wait forever
and that one day, like the geese,
she'd be gone.

Think of You and Me Together

We find a piece of the ocean
but do not know how to behave.

We are meant for the conscious life, you and I
not fully knowing that dry suits always leak.

We dive—

The shape of any wave is affected by the depth of the sea.

Peacock Feathers

Her grandfather said
it's bad luck to have them in the house.
Her grandmother kept them
in a black porcelain vase
in the hallway
right by the door.

She thought of strangers
with broken down shoes,
of the flower stickers
people adhered to their windows in Greece
so no one would walk through glass,
of men dressing in the dark,
of those who fear coffee as poison,
leaving everything for later,
growing old waiting.
Let them sob and sob
their children going to school
with lunch boxes filled with stones
opalescent women
getting gassed in their own houses.

What bad things could ever happen to us,
Karen wondered.

My Love Affair with Gertrude Stein

Carl Von Linné was born in the village of Stenbrohult, in Småland, in 1707.

Do you ever think of me when you're alone, drinking whiskey?

In the autumn of 1727, he went to Uppsala University, tucked in a sleepy hamlet on the North Baltic coast surrounded by a herbarium of 3,000 species.

Have you ever thought of me while you're having sex with someone else?

Walking in the spruce forests along the Baltic coastline with a vasculum, a field microscope, a pair of magnifying glasses, notepaper, a butterfly net, insect pins and pocket-knives.

Did I turn your life upside down, even for one day?

He discovered a botanical code, which necessitated a rigorous separation between essence and epithet.

Can you go back and tell me why you've been angry for so long or are you so tired with me you won't even leave your chair?

Without the binary denomination the generic name would be a 'bell without a clapper', Linnaeus said and in 1753 he was awarded the Swedish Order of the Polar Star.

Do you have a structure as a lover?
Every carpet has its weave, every heat parches the lawn, every time you draw back a woman's blouse there is a spine to press—a series of vertebra from the skull to the small of the back, little bones with different names.

Bedtime

The day is carried into memory
like limestone quarried into building blocks.
Anything could go wrong now—
people don't stay in bed all day, do they?

She knows some impurities can make water clearer
she knows knowledge is a door both open and closed
that love happens in the head
that time was regulated by the seasons of agriculture.

Don't be scared, her mother used to say,
Our house is full of noises.
What you hear at night is the clock and the fridge
and the plumbing and the heat—
You're not in danger.

Whist Holiday

It wouldn't rain.
She knew because the swallows were flying too high.
She was feeding birds in the garden staring at the sky,
her bicycle propped against the fence.
The cliffs nearby were falling into the sea.
The future wouldn't happen.
Three days of whist in a hotel on the coast.
Cards in the lounge near the seafront,
the rope and hauled-up fishing boats.
Every year, taking advantage of the low-season prices.
And then back home.
The wind, the gulls, the sound of water.
Another small town on the edge of the Atlantic
without a sea wall.

Her mother said if a child washed his hands
he could eat with kings.
Her mother who always made the same cake,
the one whose recipe was on the flour box.

She said to herself, go, begin, do what you have to do.
A red bicycle gleaming against the grass.
She could go anywhere—
there was something about the ocean she could not fix.
It was worth leaving home for—
three days of whist in a hotel on the coast.

If she didn't come back the way she went,
the future would happen.

Doing Things Slowly

The prince in the old story, disguised in old clothes
walks around to find out what his kingdom is really like—
the tender headlock of the sea
the waste of crimson with miles of blue sky
the slow-footed tortoises that never arrive.

The pulse of the blood, the pulse of the heart
becoming a deep dark woods
she recognizes the smell
from her grandmother's dining room
always with the shutters down
so the sun would not ruin the furniture.

Take care now Karen,
take care.

The Heimlich Manoeuvre

Stand behind the person
and wrap your arms around their waist.
Form a fist and place the thumb side of it
against the person's upper abdomen,
above the navel and below the ribcage.
Anything could happen now.

Grab your fist with your other hand
and make a quick upward thrust.
Repeat until the object blocking the airway
is dislodged.

The only way to get home is by longing
so this is how it could be

There is no muddle in us
there is a place we never leave
this is not exhausting
and you're talking to me.

Rue de Rivoli

The light crashing down the columns,
the marble on the pavement,
the chocolate éclair,
the black coffee—
Find out how best to live.

She draws a line in her notebook but
a true line has no end.

From the window of the café,
a patch of frozen blue sky.

Eclipses of the sun occur
only when three bodies are in a straight line.
It is so simple that if she is not careful, she will forget—
What happens if suddenly the shadows in the garden freeze?

The light crashing down her spine,
the éclair, the books, the columns,
opposite the window Le Jardin des Tuileries,
Hotel Le Meurice at the end of the street.

How Does Love End

With hundreds of brown paper bags filled with air.

The frozen air that the whales are said to carry in their tails,
bringing the cold from the Arctic Ocean.
A squeeze of the hand,
the knee which doesn't move away.

Democritus of Abdera tore his eyes out in a garden
so that the spectacle of reality would not distract him.

The rain
stowing the bicycles
shutting the garage doors
calling the children in.
Everything that happens but will not stay.

Extreme Unction

I'll tell you all about the battle of Copenhagen
Why Nelson disregarded Hyde Parker's signal to disengage.
I'll teach you the names of plants
Show you how to smash a pomegranate
Without missing a single seed.

Turn off the lights
Light up a candle and give me your hands
I will be wearing kneepads and orange earmuffs
and signal to your plane
I will vaporize into little pockets of oxygen
Between the limestone crags.
I will look through every window
In every house
To see what other people's lives are like.

Bergmann's Rule

Siberian tigers are bigger than Bengal tigers
and Bengal tigers are bigger
than those in equatorial jungles.
Forget the tiger.
Take the bear.

Polar bears are larger than spectacled bears
which live closer to the equator.
Take turtles and salamanders,
they tend to follow the rule,
with exceptions concentrated in lizards and snakes.
Forget the exceptions—
take what you need.
You can do anything if you're not in a hurry.

German biologist Karl Bergmann
studied animal patterns
deep into the night.
With blue lines round his eyes
he published his observations in 1847
and they became a rule.
Animals in cold climates are bigger
than their warm-climate cousins—
These are the comforts of neat enclosure.

Other people can lie if they want—but not you.
Think that equatorial animals
are supposed to be smaller,
Arctic animals larger.
Focus on the rule.

Red Queen to Alice

Who said that the character of modern life
is that everything falls apart.

Go back to that place
where the air smells of mayweed and cut grass.
Make your way through the morning
forget the Chinese whispers of cliffs
forget the dreams where
trees and chess pieces are flying through the air.

The world turns eau-de-nil.
The spruce and the hemlock hanging with moss
the deep forest with the strange animal squeaks
and the sappy, spicy smell of Sweet William
then Irish monks following Arctic geese north, towards
snow-covered black spruce and frozen tundra.

September 1st, 1923

To show you the world, I'll take you by the hand on a clear September day in Tokyo in 1923, towards the middle of the morning, when people hurry home for lunch.

To answer if there is anything that wouldn't come undone, I'll point to the ground, which begins to tremble and shake, to the cracks tearing it apart.

To dispel your disbelief, I'll take you through the people running for safety, some already buried as houses fall down, gas pipes breaking, fire spreading through the town.

The past is a dishevelled lake after a summer storm. Clear on the surface but in its depths, murky and dark.

In order not to scare you I called the frigid, ghostly lake-water, the passage of time.

The Just So People

It doesn't take tectonic shifts to bring you to life.
Sea, paper and sun, a series of nosebleeds and lots of sky.
So don't you care how I live?

There is something bottomless and eternal in heavy rain
yet nothing is ever immense unless it concerns you.
Nature gesticulates.
It does not speak.
You do not exist, but then again you do—
beyond the depth and the damage of being alive.

Winds are gusting to forty knots
the weather has no end—
he is an eternal prisoner with hooks instead of hands.

So stay a little mad.
You're right here and there is blood between us.
So you do care how I live.

The Watchtower

I am up here
it is raining
I see a cistern with a turtle in it.
This is our life.
I slip down a rung
then another.
This is when accidents happen.

The cistern rotates and departs at a slow canter.
Head, limbs and tail withdraw
into the leathery shell of the turtle.
There is rain on my hands
I run towards the sea
there is nowhere else to go.

Karen & the Scorpion

Hey Karen, you're walking on and on.
You're a bag of nerves.
All bone and beak, complexion peaches-and-cream,
your eyes thin and watery
each carrying within a print of a bird's foot.
There are quicker, deeper lives in you
like antlers littering the forest floor.
How come you never touch them?
And those sleep grains on your lids
how very much they upset me.
Glacial ice contains no salt.
There's nothing to rub on your wounds
but remember
to catch the dripping tallow
you must learn perspective drawing.

Come with me and see the world—
wild hippos cruising at night
geese being fed on fish waste.
Come and live with me in a bungalow
high above the Indian Ocean.
Life is much diminished on the coast of East Africa;
I believe you will like that.
You and I can take a lot of discomfort together.
The early light of the river broken by
the hyena's howling.
Candlesticks and sugar-bowls being polished
without any consolation.
You are the Yellow Emperor, my darling,
a novel in broken lines.
On a count of ten I'll race you to the water—
we won't even wait for the birds to settle.

How to Boil an Egg

Remove your egg from the fridge 15 mins before you wish to cook it.

There is a story about a small girl lost in a blizzard in the Alps. When she was more dead than alive, a St. Bernard arrived with a keg of brandy around his neck. The dog then attacked and ate her.

Take a small saucepan, fill with enough water to cover the egg by one centimetre and bring this to a stable simmering point.

No one will ever love you passionately for being nice.

Lower the egg into the water gently and simmer for exactly one minute.

There is no sense in sexual desire.

Remove the pan from the heat, put a lid on and leave the egg in for 6 mins for a runny yolk and 7 for a creamy yolk.

In a quiet, compliant life, wild birds in the house are seen as portents of bad news but there are no such lives.

Peel off the shell and enjoy.

Intimacy is not a fusion but a conversation.

Ink, Paper & the Black Forest

Karen reads a lot of books.
She frets a lot
and lets the wine go to her head.
She is reading while preparing
for something that will never arrive.
She is like Carlyle
who wrote fifty volumes on the value of silence.
Her life is made out of ink and paper.
The chewing of the cud
all that grass passing through her body
she'll turn it into milk.
It has to do with one's mood.

Her life is a humid forest.
Her mind made up of white pine, oak and elm.
Her voice full of branches.

She lives among black spruce and hemlock in the Black Forest
smokes salmon in an old shed after soaking it in rum
using strong carbolic soap to clean her shed.
She doesn't talk much.
There are cold sores at the corners of her mouth.
Her cottage smells of coffee, rubber and rain.
Stay where you are, I tell her with my eyes.
Don't go and waste what's best in you.
Noli me tangere, she replies.

The Scar

Together we looked for gold at the bottom of streams.
You told me there is no thunder in winter,
that it is water baobab trees store in their trunks,
and I said I see a tiled depth in every feeling,
the richest blue.

You said the heat makes the corn grow and I said
I'll spend the rest of my life
just watching things grow then
and because I was happy
you said the sorrow in my eyes
was amplified into solemn pines.

Just count the days I'm gone, you replied.
I started to try to undo time
watching the light angling across the ice.

These days you keep saying
you and I are people with blemishes
that we will go far in order to continue living
and I take heart baby
I take heart.

Beaufort Scale

Zero, a picture showing smoke rising from a chimney unperturbed
One, light air, the smoke drifting to one side
Two, light breeze, leaves meandering on the ground
Three, gentle breeze, a flag flapping
Four, moderate breeze, a tree slightly shaken
Five, fresh breeze, same tree shaken even harder
Six, strong breeze, all the leaves in the tree blown to one side
Seven, near gale, a man's umbrella blown in reverse
Eight, gale, tiles flying off a roof
Nine, strong gale, branches snapping from trees
Ten, storm, trees falling down
Eleven, violent storm, houses tumbling down
Twelve, hurricane, everything falling apart.

Für Elise

She played it badly but she kept going
and bit by bit she brought it to life.
There was something in it she needed very much
all wheels must have a hub,
all lives must have a centre and a history
or else nothing holds together.

These were strange, breathless days.
She ran in a pinewood waiting for everything to begin
she waited forever
and while a woman was sunning the mattresses,
someone was playing the piano,
always the same beginning,
the air smelled of minerals like a lake
while with her eyes closed she began building things
piece by piece until one day they stood complete.

She still hears it lingering on the rim of things,
muffled in cotton, then coming apart like wet bread.
Her parents' Steinway is sold and so is the house.
She often has to remind herself that her name is not Elise
that this is just an old piece of music
what if she keeps hearing notes in her head
what if she didn't always find the switch
in every dark room she entered?
Who knows when a life is truly over?

Only a Diamond Can Scratch a Diamond

How much more do you pull along
trying to take only one
I need to know how much more.

Inside this world there is another one
where even smelling salts don't work
where you can neither hold on to anything
nor ever see the wind
since no emotion is final.

So what is the only thing you know with certainty
about twenty thousand days?
What can it be?

Why We Take the Train

If I am a whisky glass
you're not a gushing person—

if I tell you we can cure anything by crushing herbs
that grow in the desert
you say *I see what you mean* and smile.

If I say I am soothed by the steam pipes lining the corridors
you say words have knives stuck into their waistbands.

If life is one damn thing after another
we can take it all away piece by piece.

Like the cook who finds the coldest nook in the kitchen
to keep the apples
we'll scale a cliff to the bed of an ancient lake
and track down a space to write on.

And we will take the heart out of a fish for ink
and the phosphorus will make this possible
and we will want all of life
to be like this.

How Can You Ever Leave Anything Behind

Whatever contains a variable, I do not understand.
Fresh water feels colder than salt water.
Fog and rain do not go together.
A tree grows towards the sun.

So tell me what is most important to you.
You have a blade of grass in your mouth
the streets are strewn with sand and spruce twigs
I think I know what you want—
do tell me what is most important to you.

There are no alligators in the sewers, it's only us.
What contains a variable, I do not understand—
into which goes all that I love.

Come Sit with Us and Die a Little

We have books and friends who are not here.
No one taught us how to break horses.

They say cripples do not mock cripples
but we know a little about drowning.
It's like having water on the knee—
the best things found in the wrong places.

We Have No Small Talk. None.

Each one of us a little souvenir
a penguin on a block of ice
watching frost shapes veering away.

What is stillness then
if not life listening to itself?
And what is the wind, what is it?

You Can Finally Stop Being Mad

You are homesick
without wanting to go home.
Your past lives chloroformed
you no longer have a kind word for anyone.

A life without upset
is rainfall collected in cisterns.

The world is a dark sound
the only light the glow of a ferry.
We only know how to make small worlds—
you thought of putting yours
in a biscuit tin
hiding it in a tree.
You need a bigger box
a splintered tea chest
a bigger life.

Goodbye Karen

Hotel-Echo-Yankee
Bravo-Alpha-Bravo-Yankee
India
Charlie-Alpha-November-Tango
Delta-Oscar
Tango-Hotel-India-Sierra
Alpha-November-Yankee
Mike-Oscar-Romeo-Echo

Acknowledgements

Grateful acknowledgement is made to the editors of the following publications in which some of these poems first appeared:

In the USA:
Bateau Press: 'How to boil an egg'.
BOMB Magazine Word Choice: 'Whist Holiday'.
Conjunctions: 'The Little Blind Girls,' 'One Chair,' 'The Book of Recondite Facts'.
Denver Quarterly: 'Bergmann's Rule,' 'Housekeeping,' 'The Earring,' 'Dead Man's Fingers'.
Everyday Genius: 'The Man in Chamonix'.
Folly: 'In the Fitting-Room,' 'Looking for Denys,' 'Oh, Mr. Stevens!'.
Hawaii Pacific Review: 'The Glasgow Coma Scale'.
The Healing Muse: 'Dear Miss Elspeth,' 'The Boat Accident,' 'Rue de Rivoli,' 'Until Sunday'.
KNOCK: 'A few days later'.
The Literary Review: 'The Just So People'.
Memoir (and): 'Relative Velocity'.
Nashville Review: 'September 1st 1923'.
New Delta Review: 'Amy & the Scorpion';
The New Republic: 'The Music-Box Manufacturer'.
The Normal School: 'The Scar'.
Open Letters Monthly: 'The Drifter'.
Quiddity International Literary Journal and Radio Program: 'Harbors,' 'Peanuts,' 'The Welder'.
The Raintown Review: 'Give Us'.
Rosebud Magazine: 'Eleven Things You Don't Know';
St. Ann's Review: 'Enigma'.
Salamander: 'Blue Peter'.
6 x 6: 'The Life of Explorers'.
Small Spiral Notebook: 'Coney Island'.
The South Carolina Review: 'Aeolus'.
Tampa Review: 'December'.

In the UK:
The Coffee House: 'The Caul'.
Fire: 'The Yellow Hand,' 'Indigo Snake'.
Iota: 'The Polymath'.
Magma: 'A loaf of bread and a newspaper,' 'Naming Things'.
MsLexia: 'These are fleeting thoughts'.
Oxford Poetry: 'Kayak Anxiety'.
Poetry Review: 'Caramel'.
Tears in the Fence: 'Girls who are never asked to dance,' 'Why we take the train'.

In Australia:
Wet Ink: 'The Mistake Bird'.

www.mediterranean.nu: 'The Capri Notebook,' 'Promenade des Anglais'.

My title comes from Leo Tolstoy's *Anna Karenina*: the scene where
Lyovin, with a piece of chalk, wrote the initial letters on a card-table
for Kitty Shcherbatski.

'The Riddle' is inspired by an incident in Karen Blixen's *Out of Africa*.

The quote from Ovid is from *Remedia Amoris*.

The phrases 'Begin at the Beginning' and 'Red Queen to Alice' are from
Lewis Carroll's *Alice in Wonderland*.

'A life is a life is a life' is after Gertrude Stein's a rose is a rose is a rose.

Gatsby and Daisy refer of course to F. Scott Fitzgerald's *The Great
Gatsby*.

"Due to lack of interest tomorrow has been cancelled" comes from
graffiti in a coffee house restroom in Berkeley, CA.

"It's better with the cracks" is a phrase used by Marcel Duchamp.

Mr. Crusoe senior refers to Robinson Crusoe's father in the novel by
Daniel Defoe.

Grammatical clarifications come from *The Chicago Manual of Style*,
15th edition.

It was Karl Marx who said that the character of modern life is that
everything falls apart.

Noli me tangere is Latin for "Do not touch me", which Jesus is reported
to have said to Mary Magdalene when she recognized him after his
resurrection (John 20:17).

Für Elise refers to the piece for solo piano by Beethoven.

'Goodbye Karen' is written in code based on the *NATO Phonetic
Alphabet*.

I am indebted to my allies *extraordinaires,* Arianna Culucundis, Katerina
Dafermou, Maria Kokkou, Elina Kountouri, Christianna Mira, Stephanie
Whitten.

This book is dedicated to my mother, Sophia, and in memory of my
grandparents, Athena & Petros Angelopoulos.

CPSIA information can be obtained at www.ICGtesting.com
Printed in the USA
BVOW02s2055030913

330207BV00001BA/14/P